NIGERIA
the land

Anne Rosenberg

A Bobbie Kalman Book

The Lands, Peoples, and Cultures Series

Crabtree Publishing Company
www.crabtreebooks.com

The Lands, Peoples, and Cultures Series

Created by Bobbie Kalman

Coordinating editor
Ellen Rodger

Project development, photo research, and design
First Folio Resource Group, Inc.
Erinn Banting
Pauline Beggs
Tom Dart
Kathryn Lane
Claire Milne
Debbie Smith

Editing
Jessica Rudolph

Separations and film
Embassy Graphics

Printer
Worzalla Publishing Company

Consultants
Ibrahim Hamza, York University; Olatunji Ojo, York University

Photographs
Corbis/Paul Almasy: p. 20 (right); Tim Davis, The National Audubon Society Collection/Photo Researchers: p. 28 (top); Nigel J. Dennis, The National Audubon Society Collection/ Photo Researchers: p. 31 (top); emeagwali.com: p. 21 (bottom right); W. K. Fletcher, The National Audubon Society Collection/Photo Researchers: p. 31 (bottom right); Thomas D. W. Friedman/Photo Researchers: p. 21 (top right); Georg Gerster/Photo Researchers: p. 19 (top), p. 21 (left); Lori Hale: p. 5 (bottom), p. 8 (top); Juliet Highet/ Hutchison Library: p. 3, p. 12 (top), p. 14 (top), p. 15 (top), p. 16 (top); Eric and David Hosking, The National Audubon Society Collection/Photo Researchers: p. 30 (bottom); The Hutchison Library: title page, p. 6, p. 8 (bottom), p. 13 (both), p. 18, p. 19 (bottom), p. 23 (top left), p. 24 (both), p. 25 (top); Roderick Johnson/ Panos Pictures: p. 26 (top);

Jason Lauré: p. 10 (both); George D. Lepp, The National Audubon Society Collection/Photo Researchers: p. 30 (top); S. R. Maglione, The National Audubon Society Collection/ Photo Researchers: p. 28 (bottom); Eric Miller/Lauré Communications: p. 5 (top left), p. 20 (left); Giles Moberly/ Impact: p. 12 (bottom); James Morris/Panos Pictures: p. 7 (bottom), p. 16 (bottom); Rex Parry/Panos Pictures: p. 23 (top right); Bruce Paton/Panos Pictures: p. 11 (top); Giacomo Pirozzi/Panos Pictures: p. 22 (top); Betty Press/ Panos Pictures: p. 4, p. 15 (bottom), p. 25 (bottom); Carl Purcell, The National Audubon Society Collection/ Photo Researchers: p. 11 (bottom); Diane Rawson/Photo Researchers p. 17 (top); David Reed/Panos Pictures: p. 26 (bottom); Gary Retherford, The National Audubon Society Collection/Photo Researchers: p. 27 (left); Marcus Rose/ Panos Pictures: p. 9 (bottom), p. 14 (bottom); Candace Scharsu: p. 5 (top right), p. 17 (bottom); Dr. Nigel Smith/ The Hutchison Library: p. 22 (bottom); Steinhart Aquarium, The National Audubon Society Collection/ Photo Researchers: p. 31 (bottom left); Anna Tully/The Hutchison Library: cover, p. 7 (top), p. 9 (top), p. 23 (bottom right); Art Wolfe/Photo Researchers: p. 27 (right), p. 29

Map
Jim Chernishenko

Illustrations
Dianne Eastman: icon
David Wysotski, Allure Illustrations: back cover

Cover: A group of huts crowd a hillside village near Lagos, in southern Nigeria.

Title page: A son helps his father untangle a net on their fishing boat on the Niger River.

Icon: The tower of an oil rig appears at the head of each section.

Back cover: Bush babies live in Nigeria's rainforests and savannas.

Published by
Crabtree Publishing Company

PMB 16A	612 Welland Avenue	73 Lime Walk
350 Fifth Avenue	St. Catharines	Headington
Suite 3308	Ontario, Canada	Oxford OX3 7AD
New York	L2M 5V6	United Kingdom
N.Y. 10118		

Cataloging in Publication Data
Rosenberg, Anne, 1964–
    Nigeria, the land / Anne Rosenberg.
        p. cm. -- (The lands, peoples, and cultures series)
    Includes index.
    ISBN 0-86505-247-6 -- ISBN 0-86505-327-8 (pbk.)
        1. Nigeria--Description and travel--Juvenile literature. [2. Nigeria--Juvenile literature. I. Title. II. Series.

DT515.27 .R67 2000
966.9--dc21   00-043224
                                                              LC

Contents

The Giant of Africa

In Nigeria, camels are used as a means of transportation and as a way to move goods from place to place.

South of the Sahara Desert lies a land some call "The Giant of Africa." That giant is Nigeria, one of the largest countries in West Africa and the most populated country on the African continent. People have lived in "The Giant of Africa" for thousands of years, though Nigeria only became an independent country in 1960.

Nigeria is a country blessed with plentiful **natural resources** such as oil and tin. It is also a land of great winding rivers, lush rainforests, spectacular steep cliffs, and wide-open grasslands. These varied landscapes make "The Giant of Africa" a place of incredible beauty.

Facts at a glance

Official name: Federal Republic of Nigeria

Capital city: Abuja

Population: 108 million

Area: 356,664 square miles (924,000 square kilometers)

Main languages: English, Hausa, Igbo, and Yoruba

Main religions: Islam, Christianity, and traditional beliefs

Currency: Naira

National holiday: October 1

Drill pipes are attached to a crane by workers on an oil rig. Oil is a major resource in Nigeria.

A woman helps weed a community garden in Katsina, in northern Nigeria.

A group of boys gather on a field in a village near Lagos.

A diverse land

The Niger River is 2,600 miles (4,200 kilometers) long. It flows through the countries of Guinea, Mali, Niger, and Benin before reaching Nigeria.

Nigeria is a land of contrasts. In the south, there are huge rainforests and coastal swamps. They cover the area where the Niger River meets the Atlantic Ocean. Mountains and highlands rise along the eastern border. The north is mostly flat, with occasional cliffs that drop sharply to the land below.

So much water

The Niger River is one of the longest rivers in the world. It flows through many neighboring countries before reaching Nigeria, where the Benue River joins it from the east. The Niger River flows over flat land, so it moves very slowly. During the rainy season, however, rain falls quickly and heavily. The river often floods, washing out bridges and uprooting trees. These trees then float down the rushing river, crashing into buildings at the river's edge and causing terrible damage.

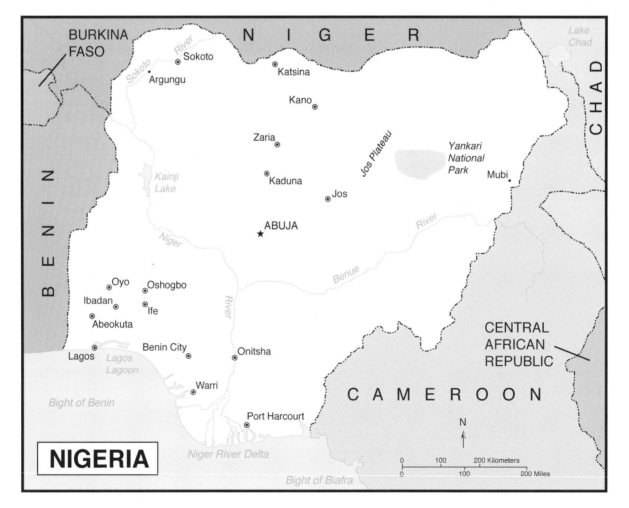

Where land and rivers meet

The coastal area in the southern part of the country is called the Niger River Delta. A river delta is an area of land that forms at the mouth of a river because of a build-up of sand and rock, carried there by the **current** over hundreds of years. Sometimes, the current is so powerful that it creates piles of sand, called sandbars, so high that boats cannot **navigate** the waterways.

The Niger River Delta is full of beaches, lagoons, creeks, and swamps. Mangrove trees grow in the swamps, extending hundreds of thick, twisted roots far beneath the ground.

Oil palm trees grow along the banks of the Lagos Lagoon on the west coast of Nigeria.

The Seven Stream Falls, in southern Nigeria, is a cataract, or large waterfall, which is made up of smaller waterfalls, called cascades.

Towering trees

Stretching northward from the coast are enormous rainforests with trees that grow over 100 feet (30 meters) high. **Cacao** trees, which supply cacao beans, the source of chocolate, are plentiful. So are trees such as mahogany, iroko, and obeche, which provide valuable hardwood for making furniture. Hundreds of animals, including monkeys, lizards, **geckos**, and fruit bats, make these forests their home.

A dry, flat landscape

Just north of the rainforest, in the middle of the country, is the **savanna**. Lions, leopards, and gazelles roam over vast areas of flat land covered with coarse grasses and scattered trees. Most of Nigeria's food crops, such as beans, rice, corn, tomatoes, and onions, grow in this area.

The flat, desert-like savanna extends as far as the eye can see.

A village sits in a valley near the city of Ibadan, in western Nigeria.

Plains and plateaus

A large section of northern Nigeria is formed by stretches of flat land, called plains. Scattered on the plains are tall, rocky formations called *inselbergs* that are created by the wind and rain wearing away layers of rock. The north also consists of plateaus, or areas of flat land that stand higher than the surrounding land. The highest of these is the Jos Plateau. It rises to a height of 4,000 feet (1,280 meters). Many people live here because of its **fertile** farmland and rich mineral resources.

(right) The Nsukka River, which feeds into the Niger River, provides a water source for the city of Onitshain in southern Nigeria.

(below) The enormous Aesop Rock looms above a highway on the outskirts of Abuja, Nigeria's capital.

Weather report

Nigeria has two main seasons: a rainy season and a dry season. The rainy season lasts longer in southern Nigeria than in the northern part of the country. The Jos Plateau, in the center of Nigeria, has the mildest climate, making it a popular vacation spot.

Drought

Water becomes very precious in the summer, when the temperature can climb as high as 120° Fahrenheit (48° Celsius). In some villages, people say prayers to bring rain. When no rain falls for a long period, it is called a drought. During a drought, vegetables and other wildlife do not grow, and water supplies dry up. Nigeria has experienced long periods of drought, when food and water had to be brought from other countries to help the people survive.

(right) A truck gets stuck on a muddy road after a heavy rainfall.

(below) Plants and palm trees wither during a period of drought in the north.

The people of Kaduna, in northern Nigeria, dig a hole in the hopes of finding water deep underground.

Disappearing land

When the earth's surface is worn away by rain or wind, the effect is called erosion. During the wet season, Nigeria's heavy rainfall erodes some of its land formations. On the Jos Plateau, the rainfall creates deep gullies that cut through the earth. In the southern part of Nigeria, the heavy rain washes away entire hillsides!

Cover your eyes!

Between October and March, dry air from the Sahara Desert pushes the moist air over Nigeria into the Atlantic Ocean. People refer to this dry air as the harmattan wind. It brings very hot weather during the day and very cold temperatures at night. It also carries large amounts of dust. Sometimes, the air is filled with so much dust that planes are unable to take off because the pilots cannot see.

A fast-approaching dust storm blows across the Niger River.

A land of many peoples

(left) This Igbo man lives in Benin City, in southern Nigeria.

(below) A Yoruba potter makes a bowl out of clay.

During its long history, Nigeria was a **crossroads** for travelers. Many different peoples settled there. Today, the country is home to over 470 **ethnic groups**, each with its own language, beliefs, and customs. The Hausa and the Fulani peoples are the largest groups in northern Nigeria. In the southern part of the country, the largest groups are the Yoruba in the west and the Igbo in the east. Over the years, Nigeria's ethnic groups have had many religious and political differences, which led to conflicts and **civil war.** For the past two decades, Nigerians have been working hard to keep their fragile peace.

The Igbo

The Igbo are a mix of almost 200 smaller groups. Historians are not certain where they first came from, but they believe that the Igbo have lived in the southeast part of Nigeria for about 5,500 years. The Igbo became skilled blacksmiths, who spread their knowledge of iron-working techniques throughout Africa. Most Igbo are Christians. They follow the teachings of Jesus Christ, who Christians believe is the son of God.

The Yoruba

The Yoruba first came to the land around 100 B.C. Many more arrived between the years 800 and 1200 A.D. Today, the Yoruba live in densely populated cities, where many work as **artisans**, exchanging their home-made crafts for **textiles** and other goods. Most Yoruba are Christians or Muslims. Muslims follow the religion of Islam. They believe in one god, called Allah, and follow the teachings of his **prophet**, Muhammad. Some Yoruba continue to observe their traditional religious practices, which involve praying to hundreds of gods and goddesses.

The Hausa

The Hausa first settled in Nigeria between 1000 and 1100 A.D. Most big cities in northern Nigeria have a Hausa community, or *zango*. *Zango* originally referred to a stopping point for trading caravans, the groups of **merchants** who rode across West Africa. At the ancient *zango*, the Hausa traded goods in exchange for **kola** nuts and salt. Today, many Hausa are still traders, selling their merchandise to local villagers and tourists. Most Hausa are Muslims.

The Fulani

The Fulani, or Fulbé as some people call them, first arrived in Nigeria around 1200 A.D. Most Fulani live in Nigeria's cities. The **pastoral** Fulani live in villages in the countryside for part of the year. They move away from their homes during the dry season in search of good grazing land for their cattle. Both groups of Fulani are Muslims, but the Fulani who live in cities follow Muslim practices much more strictly than the pastoral Fulani do.

(above) Three young Hausa women show off their new dresses outside a market stall.

(below) A group of Fulani women and children wait for a bus to take them home after a busy day at the market.

Nigeria's cities

In the past, most Nigerians lived in rural areas, where they farmed or fished for a living. Today, the cities are becoming busier as people move from the countryside to search for work.

Lagos

The city of Lagos is built on a series of islands. Portugese explorers gave the city its name, which means "lagoon," because of the swamps and lagoons that surround it. There are four parts to the city: the three islands of Lagos, Ikoyi, and Victoria, and the mainland area, which is also called Lagos.

The former **capital** of Nigeria, Lagos has long been the country's main port and business center. This modern city is crowded with skyscrapers and office buildings. On the main roads, bustling markets and shops sell spices, perfumes, colorful silks, and velvets. Trucks weave through the city's busy streets, competing for space with cars, buses, and people on their way to work. Sidewalk vendors take advantage of the frequent traffic jams, selling soft drinks and snacks to drivers stuck in what Nigerians call "go slows."

Hundreds of merchants and shoppers crowd the busy Iddo market in Lagos.

Many new homes have been built in Abuja since it became the country's capital.

Abuja

In the late 1970s, when the city of Lagos became too crowded, the government decided to build a new capital city, Abuja. Abuja was built in the center of the country, outside the areas controlled by the major ethnic groups. This location was chosen so that the city would be neutral, not belonging to or supporting any particular group. This way, Nigerians would know that the capital belonged to them all.

When workers began construction, Abuja was completely undeveloped, without any highways or buildings. By 1991, when Abuja became the new capital, the city had shops, restaurants, courts, and government offices.

Ibadan

Ibadan was originally a fortress. It was built on a range of hills, which made it easy to defend. Today, Ibadan is a major business and agricultural center. The 25-story Cocoa House, in the central business district, was the first skyscraper in Nigeria. Palm oil and cacao, two of Nigeria's chief exports, are both produced in the city. The enormous Gbagi market is said to be the biggest market in West Africa. Shoppers can buy almost anything here — fresh vegetables, woven cloth, leather goods, and even televisions.

(above) Artisans make bowls and vases out of gourds, which are hard-shelled fruit. They will sell their wares at the market in Ibadan.

(left) An apartment building in Oshogbo, in southwest Nigeria, has huge archways, brightly painted columns, and a balcony that extends right around the building.

Benin City

Benin City dates back to the thirteenth century. Long ago, it was surrounded by a moat and wall to defend the people against outsiders. These walls have been torn down to make room for modern buildings, but the city's history can still be seen in the palace of the *Oba*, the traditional leader of Benin's kingdom. The palace is filled with beautiful bronze sculptures made for the royal court.

Kano

Founded around the ninth century, Kano is one of the oldest cities in West Africa. It is the second most important business center in Nigeria, producing dye, leather, and woven cloths. Kano is really two separate cities — an ancient city called Cikin Birni and Kano, the modern settlement. Centuries ago, Cikin Birni was surrounded by thick, clay walls with thirteen gates. Today, most of these walls have fallen down, but the gates still stand. The main gate, Kofar Mata, leads to the central mosque, the Muslim place of worship, and to a magnificent 800-year-old palace belonging to the *emir,* the Muslim ruler of the city.

This statue of the **Oba** *stands outside the traditional leader's palace in Benin City.*

Three men rest in front of a house with elaborately decorated walls in Zaria, a city in northern Nigeria.

16

Goats graze on short grass and people pass in front of the Great Mosque in Kano.

An ancient gateway still stands in the old part of Kano.

Going from place to place

People who live in Nigeria travel long distances for work and adventure. In the past, people made these long journeys by boat on the country's lakes and rivers. Now, people also use buses, trains, motorcycles, and taxis to get around.

On the water

Nigeria's waterways are an important part of the country's transportation system. For people who live in the swampy creeks and lagoons of the Niger River Delta, traveling by boat is often the only way to get around.

The Niger and Benue Rivers are Nigeria's most important inland waterways, transporting large numbers of people and goods. Today, passenger boats and steamers still sail these waters, but they now share the rivers with cruise ships and motorboats.

Animal power

In northern Nigeria's villages, where there are few paved roads, people sometimes use animals to get from place to place. They ride camels and strap donkeys to carts to transport goods. Bicycles and motorcycles are also good ways to travel on the rough dirt roads of the countryside.

By bus

Buses connect all of Nigeria's main cities. Big buses called *luxurius* are used for long-distance trips. These buses are very comfortable and well maintained.

Small buses called *danfos* are used for both long trips and for travel within a city. *Danfos* can be crowded. They are made for ten passengers, but they often carry up to sixteen.

(top) A boatman takes a mother and daughter across the Niger River while camels drink by the riverside, preparing for the long journey home.

Molue buses

In the city of Lagos, people get around in big buses called *molues*. *Molues* are always overcrowded. There is room for thirty people to travel sitting down, but *molues* usually carry twice that number. People squeeze in wherever they can find space, even if it means hanging out the door! A Nigerian song about the *molue* describes it as "Forty-four sitting, ninety-nine standing, suffering and smiling … Everyday … the same thing."

(right) A man rides a bicycle along a country road outside of Kano.

(left) A man pulling a cart filled with merchandise slows down traffic on a busy street in Ibadan.

Industry

Nigeria's largest industries are based on its natural resources such as oil, iron, and columbine, a stone used to make cement. As these industries grew, other industries, such as manufacturing, became weak. Nigerians are now developing new industries so that the country's economy does not depend solely on profits from the sale of its resources, especially oil.

Oil is discovered

In 1956, a company called Shell-British Petroleum discovered oil in the southern town of Oloibiri. Since then, oil has been Nigeria's largest industry. Earnings from it have built roads, schools, and hospitals. Today, Nigeria is the tenth-largest producer of oil in the world, turning out two million barrels every day. This oil is sold around the world, where it is used to heat houses, provide fuel for cars, and make various kinds of plastic.

A woman fills bottles of perfume at a factory in Lagos.

The Ogoni protests

Oil companies have had a devastating effect on the environment and on the people who live in the area where oil has been found. Between 1976 and 1991, over 3,000 oil spills in the area killed wildlife and destroyed the farmland of the Niger River Delta, including the land of the Ogoni people. In 1993, hundreds of thousands of Ogoni marched in peaceful protests to try to stop the damage and receive **compensation**. The military was sent in and killed or injured thousands of people. Today, many Ogoni have moved to other parts of the country, but others remain in their villages, working to see that justice is done.

Workers on an oil rig prepare to drill a well in Ogoniland, on the Niger River Delta.

Mining for tin

Tin is a soft, silvery-white metal known for its strength. It is used to make a variety of objects, from tin cans and tin foil, to cars and airplanes. Most of Nigeria's tin is found in the Jos Plateau. To remove the tin, miners aim powerful jets of water at the earth, causing the outer layer to crumble and wash away. The part that remains holds the metal.

Fishing

Nigeria's waters are home to a wide variety of fish such as sardines, mackerel, perch, and catfish. Most of the country's fish are caught along the coastal waters, but Nigerians also fish their lakes and rivers. Although there are a few large companies that use modern equipment, most Nigerian fishermen still use traditional methods such as nets and traps. Each day, they sell their catch by the side of the road. There is little electricity in rural areas, so freshly caught fish cannot be stored. They must be eaten right away or preserved by drying and salting.

Fishermen in a small village near Okene, in central Nigeria, smoke their catch on a huge clay oven.

Tin miners use shovels to loosen the soil and direct the flow of water at a mine in the Jos Plateau, in central Nigeria.

Philip Emeagwali was nicknamed "Calculus" when he was eight years old because he was such a good math student.

The computer industry

Nigeria has a growing computer industry. One Nigerian who helped develop this industry is the computer scientist and inventor Philip Emeagwali. Emeagwali invented the Connection Machine, which could solve 3.1 billion mathematical problems each second. That was a world record! Using the Connection Machine, companies have found a way to get more oil out of the ground. People around the world also use the Connection Machine to make weather predictions more accurate, to track the spread of disease, and to determine the long-term effects of pollution on the environment.

Growing crops

Nigeria's warm climate is ideal for growing a variety of fruit and vegetables. In the rainy south, sweet potatoes, **yams**, and **cassava** are common crops. In the north, where the climate is drier, the main crops are beans, such as soybeans, as well as **maize**, **millet**, and **sorghum**. Much of Nigeria's harvest is eaten by the farmers themselves or sent to outdoor markets and neighborhood shops. However, rubber, cacao, and oil palm trees are grown on huge **plantations** and their products are sold to other countries.

Family farms

Farming has been a way of life in Nigeria for centuries. Most farmers live in rural areas, but some live in cities and travel long distances to family farms in the countryside. Most of these farms are small, and the families who work the land use simple tools and animals to help with their work. The women tend the vegetable plots and care for the **livestock**, while the men plow the fields and harvest the crops. Children help by feeding the animals, carrying water, and picking fruit.

Developing fertile farmland

Some farmers grow different crops on the same land from one year to the next. For example, they might grow maize one year and beans the next. This system of farming, called crop rotation, helps keep the soil fertile. In areas where fewer people live, fields are **cultivated** for several years and then left to lie fallow, which means that no crops are planted for one or two growing seasons. When land is farmed year after year, the soil becomes exhausted, making it difficult to grow anything. When the land lies fallow, it regains moisture and **nutrients** that will help future crops.

(above) A young girl helps her mother peel and prepare cassava that will be sold at a market.

A farmer sows his land near Benin City.

Workers cut open bags of beans which they will load into a silo.

A flexible crop

Rubber comes from rubber trees, which grow in the southern part of the country. Natural rubber comes in the form of a milky white liquid called latex. To collect the rubber, farmers cut out a thin layer of bark, being careful not to damage the tree. Then, they fasten a small cup or bag to the trunk. The liquid latex drips into the cup or bag where the bark has been cut. The liquid is collected and taken to factories, where it is dried and shipped to other countries. There, this extremely strong and flexible material is used to make many different products.

An oily crop

Nigeria's oil palm trees thrive in the humid climate in the south. These trees produce red, yellow, and orange fruit in egg-shaped clusters. Each fruit is about one inch (three centimeters) long. Inside is a seed buried in a reddish pulp. The oil palm tree produces two types of oil. Palm oil, which is taken from the pulp, is used to make soap and candles. Some Nigerians smear their bodies with it so the rain rolls right off. Palm kernel oil is taken from the seeds. It has a nutty flavor, and is used to make margarine as well as soap and candles.

Latex from this tree can be used to make everyday objects such as rubber bands and tires. It can also be used to help hold up bridges and buildings.

A truckload of oil palm fruit arrives at a processing plant in Abuja.

Cotton

The cotton plant grows in the dry savanna of northern Nigeria. Cotton plants produce seeds that develop inside oval-shaped coverings called bolls. When these bolls are fully grown, they split open, revealing the seeds. The seeds are surrounded by a downy white substance, which is picked, then taken to factories and made into cloth. The cotton cloth is used to make clothes, sheets, and the brightly patterned fabrics sold in Nigeria's many markets.

People stack bags of groundnuts on top of one another to form a giant pyramid.

Chocolate, anyone?

Cacao beans grow on cacao trees, mostly in southwest Nigeria. The beans are found inside pods that are a little smaller than a football. The pods are picked and split open. Then, the beans are removed and used to make chocolate, a favorite snack.

Nuts!

Nigeria grows thousands of groundnuts, or peanuts, in the north. The seeds of the groundnut plant grow in the ground. When the plant is ripe, people pull it out by the roots and leave the nuts to dry under the hot sun. The groundnuts are then eaten or pressed for their oil, which is used in cooking.

A boy herds cattle along a road near Mubi, in northeast Nigeria.

A girl picks starfruit on a plantation near Ibadan.

Wake up!

The juice of the kola nut is an ingredient in Coca-Cola and other soft drinks. The nut is found inside the fruit of the kola tree, which grows in the southwestern part of the country. The nuts are usually white or red, and they vary in size. Nigerians often give kola nuts as a sign of friendship. Some people chew them when they are thirsty. Others chew them instead of drinking coffee since, like coffee, they have caffeine in them, which helps keep people awake.

Improving agriculture

In the past, drought severely damaged Nigeria's crops, and the country has not always been able to feed its growing population. The government is now working to improve the situation by developing irrigation projects, which help bring water to farmers' fields. It is also selling farmers **fertilizer** and seeds at low prices, so that they can produce more and better crops.

Farmers divide their fields with mounds of earth. This allows them to flood only those sections with crops that are in danger because of drought.

Animal and plant life

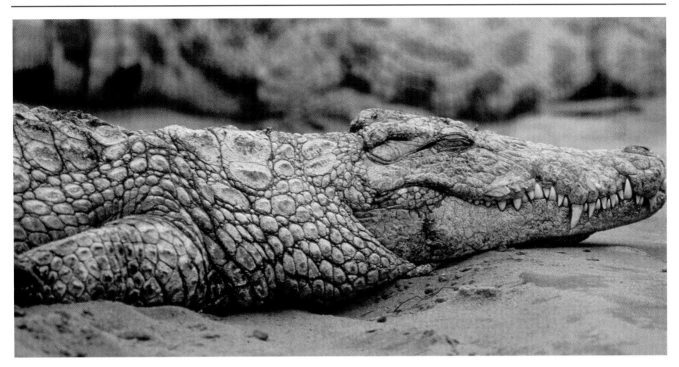

The slender-snouted crocodile can grow to be 13 feet (4 meters) long.

Nigeria's diverse environments provide a wide variety of animal **habitats**. Turtles and crocodiles swim in the swamps of the Niger River Delta. Rainforests are home to monkeys, squirrels, hawks, and fruit bats. Gazelles and elephants roam the vast grasslands of the savanna.

Crocodiles

Crocodiles live in Nigeria's swamps and slow-moving streams. When they float, most of their body remains underwater. All you can see are their eyes and nostrils sticking out! Crocodiles are among the most powerful **reptiles** in the world. They use their jaws to catch and kill their food, which is usually fish or birds. If they capture a larger animal, they use their tails to propel themselves into deep waters where they drown their prey. When they are not hunting, crocodiles spend much of the day on land with their jaws open. This is a crocodile's way of sweating. The moist surfaces in its mouth release heat, lowering its body temperature.

Hippos are vegetarians. Their diet consists of plants and grasses.

Hippopotamuses

Hippopotamuses, or river horses as they are sometimes called, look more like their distant cousins, pigs, than horses. They spend their days in lakes and rivers, coming out only at night to search for food. Their eyes sit on top of their heads, so they are able to stay underwater while keeping watch for danger. Hippos' ears and nostrils have flaps that close so the water does not get in. Using their large, curved teeth, they tear plants that they find in the river. If a male hippo meets an enemy, he bares his teeth in a fierce grin.

When bush babies call out, they sound like babies crying.

Monkeys

The rainforest is home to many types of monkeys. With their long arms and tails, monkeys are excellent climbers, swinging easily through the trees or running along the branches on all fours. The forest can be a noisy place when monkeys are around. Their shrieks echo far and wide as they warn of approaching danger.

Diana monkeys

Diana monkeys, which are named after the goddess Diana in ancient **myths**, have white hair that looks like a crown on their foreheads. Thick pads of leathery skin on their backsides create a comfortable cushion that allows them to sleep on the rough bark of trees. Their keen vision helps them find food such as grasshoppers, beetles, and butterflies.

Bush babies

African bush babies look a little like monkeys, their distant relatives. Bush babies live in the rainforest and the treed areas of the savanna. They are **nocturnal** creatures. Sleeping in nests during the day, they swing through the trees at night searching for fruit and insects to eat. Fleshy pads on their fingers and toes help them grasp the slippery branches. Their long hind legs are ideal for jumping, allowing them to escape enemies.

Sunbirds

African sunbirds make their home high above the rainforest floor. Their unusual nests look like purses hanging from trees. Sunbirds feed on insects and the sweet nectar inside flowers. They use their tongues, which are shaped like tubes, to suck up the nectar.

Armies of ants

Driver ants are just one of the many types of ants found in Nigeria. They live in underground colonies in the rainforest, sometimes with ten million ants in a colony! With so many ants living together, they quickly run out of food and must move every few days to find more. They are called driver ants because they drive over any other insect that crosses their path and tear it to pieces with their strong mandibles, or jaws.

A Diana monkey munches on small plants and insects in a rainforest.

African elephants, unlike Indian elephants, have big ears, a rounded forehead, long tusks, and a dip in their backs.

The ball python is camouflaged. Its colors help it blend in with its surroundings.

(right) The baobab tree is called the "upside-down tree" because its branches look like roots.

Elephants

There are two species of elephants: the African and the Indian. African elephants, which are larger than their Indian cousins, live in West Africa's forests and savanna. They do not live in one spot, but travel in groups called herds. These herds eat an enormous amount of leaves, twigs, tree bark, and other plants, so they have to keep moving to search for new food supplies. To drink, elephants suck water into their trunks and squirt it into their mouths. When it is hot, they use their trunks to spray themselves with water.

Ball pythons

Ball pythons are snakes that live in the rainforest and in the wetter parts of the savanna. They are good swimmers. Before entering the water, they fill their lungs with large amounts of air, which causes their lungs to inflate like balloons. This allows ball pythons to float. If ball pythons want to dive deeper, they release some of the air. Though they eat meat and can swallow their prey in one gulp, ball pythons are rarely dangerous to humans. When they sense danger from people or large animals, they roll into a tight ball and tuck their head and neck into their coiled bodies.

Baobab trees

The baobab tree grows in the dry landscape of the savanna. Its thick branches store the little rainwater that falls. This helps the tree survive in the driest weather. For Nigerians, the most important parts of the baobab tree are the leaves and fruit. The leaves are used to make soup and the fruit is mixed with milk to make delicious drinks.

Disappearing habitats

Nigeria's lush tropical forests are disappearing quickly. Logging companies clear the land for lumber to sell to other countries. Farmers cut down trees to create more farmland for crops. When the land is cleared, the soil loses important nutrients that it gets from plants and trees, making it difficult for new trees to grow. When plants and animals lose the natural habitats they need to survive, they also disappear.

Keeping the trees

There are many ways to benefit from the rainforest without destroying natural habitats. In some villages, people collect grasses, leaves, fruit, and nuts from the forest floor. These products are then eaten, used, or sold. **Conservationists** are also working to find new ways to save the rainforests. They are encouraging logging companies to leave some trees instead of clearing the land completely. Those trees that remain provide the soil with nutrients, and new trees can grow more easily.

(above) The African tulip tree grows in Nigeria's rainforests and jungles. Bats pollinate its beautiful red and orange blossoms.

(below) A palm-nut vulture takes a break from flying.

A family of zebra takes a refreshing drink at a waterhole.

Protecting Nigeria's wildlife

For many years, hunters threatened Nigeria's wildlife. Lions were killed for their hides, crocodiles were hunted for their skins, and African elephants were hunted for their ivory tusks, which were used to make carvings and jewelry. Many of these animals almost became **extinct.** The government set up two wildlife reserves to protect these animals from humans. At the Yankari and Borgu wildlife reserves, visitors can see lions, monkeys, waterbuck, and crocodiles roaming freely.

(above) A soldier commodore butterfly rests on a plant in a nature reserve in southern Nigeria.

(left) Catfish have barbels, or whisker-like extensions, around their faces that help them find food and communicate with other catfish.

31

Glossary

artisan A skilled craftsperson

cacao A type of tree that produces cacao beans, which are used to make chocolate

capital A city where the government of a state or country is located

cassava A starchy root vegetable that is shaped like a carrot

civil war A war between different groups of people or areas within a country

compensation Something given or received as payment for a loss or injury

conservationist A person who works to preserve natural resources

crossroads A place that is centrally located

cultivate To prepare land for farming by plowing or fertilizing it

current The flow of water along a certain path

ethnic group A group of people who share a common race, language, heritage, or religion

extinct No longer in existence

fertile Able to produce abundant crops or vegetation

fertilizer A substance added to the soil to make it produce more crops

gecko A small tropical lizard that has suction cups on its toes which it uses to climb trees

habitat The area or environment in which plants or animals are normally found

kola A tropical tree found in West Africa that produces nuts used to make soft drinks

livestock Farm animals

maize Corn

merchant A person who buys and sells goods

millet A type of grain

myth A traditional story about a god or another being with superhuman powers

natural resource A material found in nature such as oil, coal, minerals, or lumber

navigate To steer

nocturnal Active at night

nutrient A substance that a living thing needs in order to grow

pastoral Relating to shepherds or herders

plantation A large farm on which crops such as cotton and sugar are grown

prophet A person who is believed to speak on behalf of a god

reptile A cold-blooded animal with scales or plates covering its body

savanna A flat grassland found in tropical areas

sorghum A type of grain used to make syrup

textile A fabric or cloth

yam A type of sweet potato

Index

1 2 3 4 5 6 7 8 9 0 Printed in the USA 5 4 3 2 1 0 9 8 7 6